Think Ink
by: A J Crigler

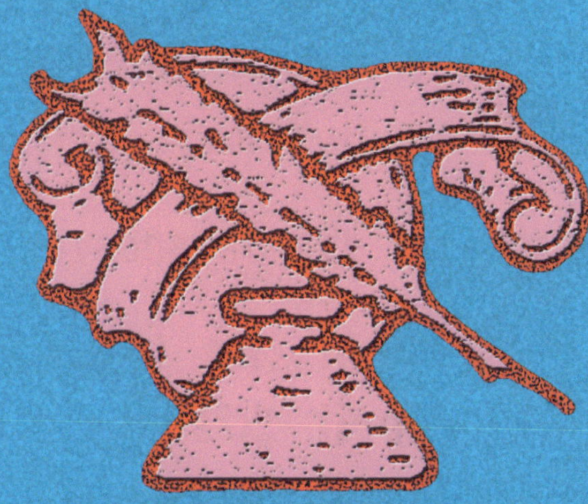

Think Ink

©2011 Aleta J. Crigler
All rights reserved.
Published by Me,
Edited by: W.R. Crigler
Co-Edited by: K.J. Crigler

ISBN-13: 978-0615803104

Printed in the U.S.A.
April 2013
original draft February 2011

Think Ink

Artwork and story by: A J Crigler
StoryTime Publications
P.O. Box 1644
Miamisburg, OH 45343-1644

Copyright © 2011 by AJ Crigler.

ISBN-13: 978-0615803104
ISBN-10: 0615803105

All rights reserved. No part of this book may be reproduced or transmitted in any form or by any means, electronic or mechanical, including photocopying, recording, or by any information storage and retrieval system, without permission in writing from the copyright owner.

This is a work of fiction. Names, characters, places and incidents either are the product of the author's imagination or are used fictitiously, and any resemblance to any actual persons, living or dead, events, or locales is entirely coincidental.

This book was printed in the United States of America.

To order additional copies of this book, contact: AJ Crigler at

www.ajcstorytimepubllications.com
email: ajcstorytimepublications@aol.com

Think Ink

Come and discover

I want you to think of ink today.

It starts with an "I" and ends with "k,"
but it works with other letters in an amazing way.

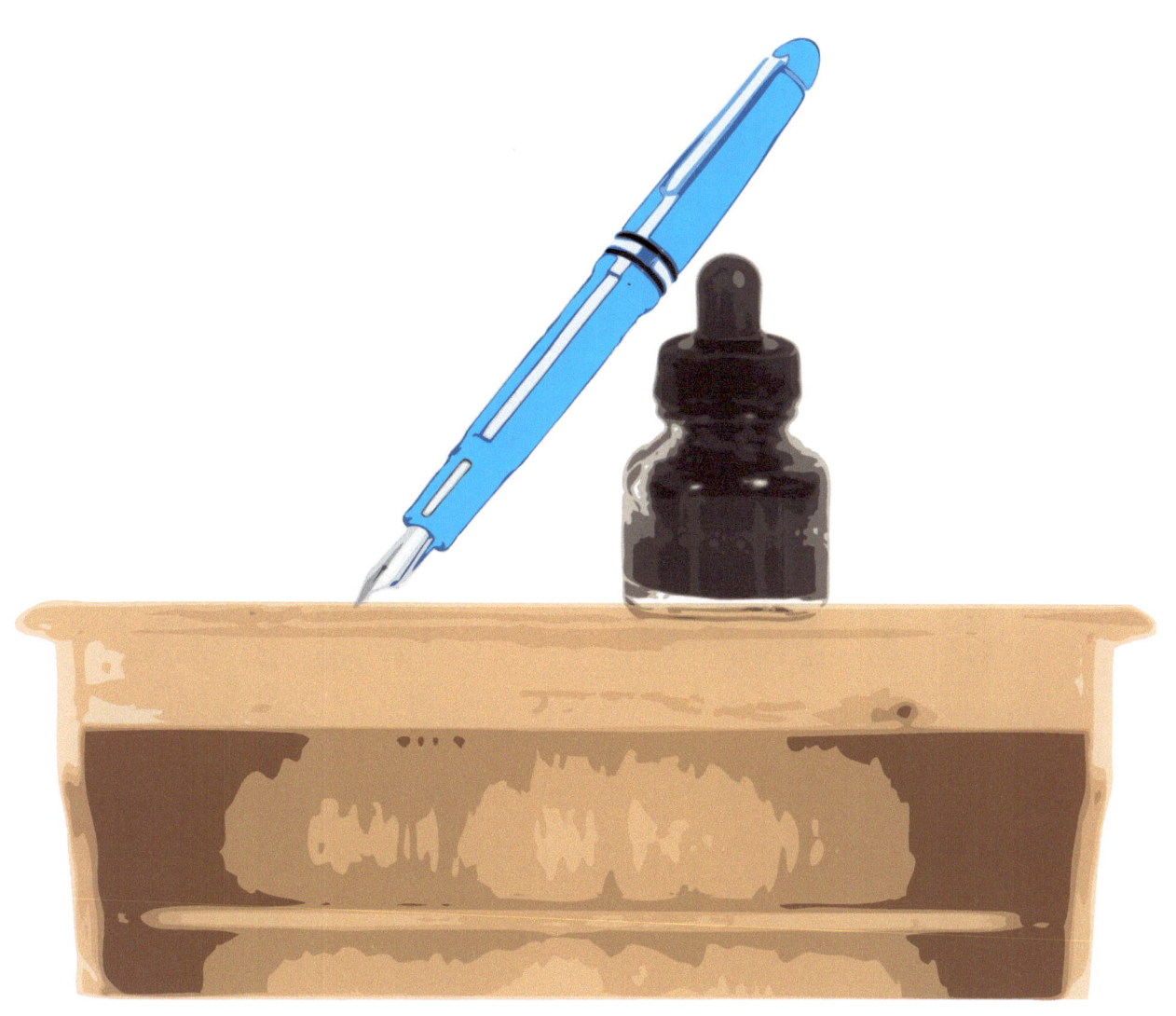

Ink can work all by itself,
in a pen, or sitting on a shelf.

Let's use "ink" after t - h to use our brains to "think."

Th ink

Just push them both together and make the two parts "link."

Now we have "link" and "think," two words that rhyme at the end.

Let's do some more and make it rhyme.
Think ink today, my friend!

Words are easy to rhyme. Come play the game, you will see.

Can you think of words that rhyme with I - N - K with me?

We started with "think," that ends with "ink" and so does the color "pink."

There are other words and we can find them, but you may miss them if you "blink."

How many have we discovered so far? Think, ink, link, pink, and then there is blink.
I know we can come up with more than that. "I know!" How about "rink?"

You can skate on a "rink." A flat surface made of ice.
So put on skates and make a figure 8; that's so nice.

If you bump your skates together you may hear a "clink."
The sound of metal touching to join
c - l with "ink."

clink

Ice is made of water that freezes at degrees below 32.
I like ice in my glass to have a frosty "drink," how about you?

I use water to wash my clothes in a washer or in the "sink."
Sweaters are sometimes hard to wash, because they often "shrink."

Try to think of more words
on your own that end with
the sound of "ink."

We have found quite a few;
and now let's review and
list them as we "rethink."

Think, ink, link, pink, and then there is blink. There is rink, clink, drink, sink, shrink, and also rethink.

I like this rhyming game; we have learned 11 words in all. I hope they stay in our brains and are there for total recall.

I thought of another word that is number 12 on our list.
It is the word "wink" and I have discovered this;
that a "wink" is a "blink," but is just a little slower.
You only use one eye and there is one eyelid to lower.

Now that we have 12 words let's recite them all again.
I think if we say them long enough we will remember them with a grin.
Think, ink, link, pink, wink, and then there is blink.
There is rink, clink, drink, sink, shrink, and also rethink.

The last word that I can **think** of that ends with the sound "**ink**,"
is a word that is unpleasant and it starts with **S - T**,
I **think**.

S - T and then I - N - K,
I think that you can tell.
It's a word that spells
something that we do not want
to smell.
This word is how we will end,
our I - N - K, rhyming fun.
When you say the word
"Stink," it is
the end
and please, do not run?

Think Ink

Artwork and Story by: A J Crigler

Think Ink

 Think ink came to me suddenly in a dream and I awakened to start writing the words that were in my head. I had been wanting to write an educational story for a while, but I was not expecting it to come the way it did. *Think Ink* is entertaining and fun for children ages 5 - 10 who are learning to read and can also be entertaining to adults that are working with them.

 I always enjoy writing stories, especially children's stories, because I know how important having good reading skills can be. This book is dedicated and is a legacy to my children and grandchildren to share the beauty of literature and the world of imagination.

www.ingramcontent.com/pod-product-compliance
Lightning Source LLC
Chambersburg PA
CBHW041230040426

42444CB00002B/117